Roundy & Friends
Book Eight

Andres Varela

Illustrations and Graphic Design by Carlos F. González
Co-Producer Germán Hernández
Third Edition
© 2019 Soccertowns® LLC

The journey around the cities where soccer is played continues as the team heads toward Boston in the State of Massachusetts.

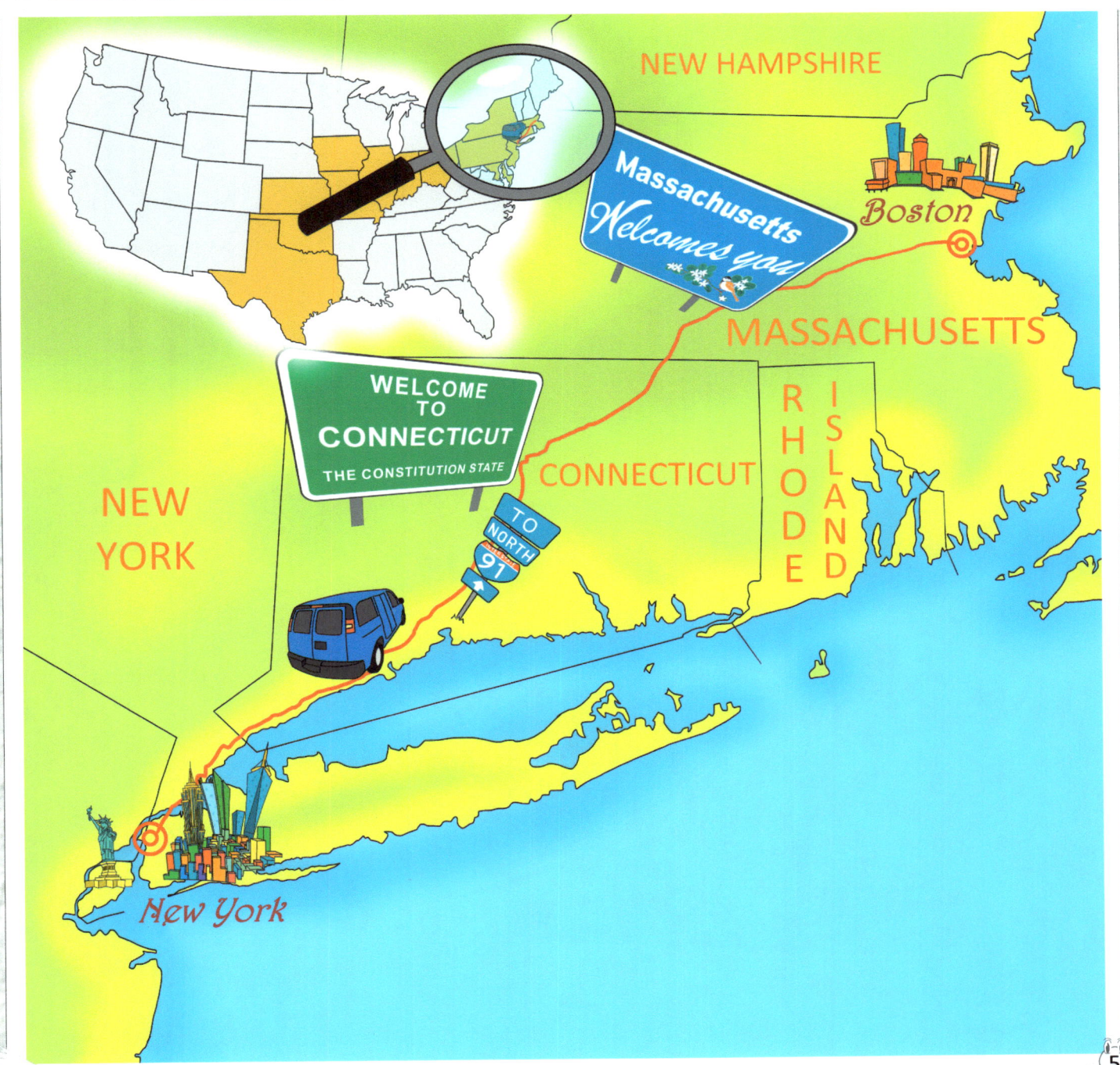

Boston is a beautiful city close to the Atlantic Ocean with over 4 Million people in the urban area.

Located on the Atlantic Coast, also called the East Coast of the United States, Boston also contains several rivers, canals and bays around the metropolitan area.

People enjoy many water sports all around the city.

There are several DUKW vehicles in Boston, currently used for touring the city. They were originally designed and used during World War II as a transportation vehicle for troops as well as other goods used during the war.
Some people call them Ducks because they can go on land and water.

Aquariums are buildings where fish, plants and other sea creatures live in see-through tanks so people can watch them swim, play and eat. Most aquariums are great sources of fun and education for children and adults.

One of this aquarium's main attractions is a transparent tunnel, where sharks, stingrays, coral reefs, octopi and many other sea creatures can be seen from every direction. While standing in it, the group sees sharks, stingrays, coral reefs, octopi and many other sea creatures.

"What are coral reefs?" asks Emma. Teo explains, "Coral reefs are a group of corals and other creatures that live in the ocean. Corals are water invertebrates, meaning animals without a vertebrate column. People have a vertebral column also known as our backbone or spine; these corals don't."

After a fun morning touring the city and learning about many plants and animals in the aquarium, they head over to one of the small ports to take a boat tour to Stellwagen Bank, an area in the Atlantic Ocean where there are many whales.
This boat will take them to see some of these beautiful whales in their natural environment.

The boat will take them on a 3 hour afternoon tour to the Bank, which is about 25 miles (40 km) east of Boston.

Once they get to the bank, they look around for whales, but 30 minutes later still no whales surfaced. Roundy kept looking in every direction because he was sure whales were going to come up. Everybody else was looking the other way when Roundy saw a gigantic whale jump out of the water, making a huge splash.

Everybody saw only the splash except Roundy who saw the whole jump. Shortly after a whole family of whales surfaced and allowed them to take some good pictures and see them in their natural habitat.

They returned to Boston very happy after such a fantastic experience!

After their long day, they head to their extended stay hotel, just like the one they stayed at in Washington D.C.

The next day, the group continued to learn about Boston as they drove through the city. They learned about a major construction project commonly known as the "Big Dig". The goal of this project was to reduce the traffic jams entering and leaving the city and to make sure more people could easily move from one point to another.

Planning on the project began in 1982, while the actual construction started in 1991 and finished in 2007. The first highways of the project opened in 2002.

Amazingly, several highways were built underneath downtown Boston. In order to do this, they had to remove several buildings and move others to different locations.

Thousands of people worked on this project during the 16 years of constructions. This is considered one of the most complicated construction projects in the history of the United States.

Underwater tunnels connecting Logan Airport to the mainland were included in the construction.

The underground highways take the group to I-93 North and then I-89 North, leading to Canada.

Boston was a lot of fun! Our Soccertowns tour is now taking us to a different country, north of the United States.

Come back and read the next story, we're heading to Canada!......

www.ingramcontent.com/pod-product-compliance
Lightning Source LLC
Chambersburg PA
CBHW041500220426
43661CB00016B/1212